The Family from Vietnam

Tana Reiff

A PACEMAKER LifeTimes™ BOOK

Fearon Education
a division of
David S. Lake Publishers
Belmont, California

LifeTimes™ Titles

So Long, Snowman
The Family from Vietnam
A Time to Choose
Mollie's Year
Juan and Lucy
A Place for Everyone
The Shoplifting Game

Editorial Director: Robert G. Bander
Managing Designer: Kauthar Hawkins
Cover, text design, and illustrations: Wayne Snyder
and Teresa Snyder

All characters herein are fictional. Any
resemblance to real persons is purely coincidental.

ISBN–0–8224–4320–1
Library of Congress Catalog Card Number:
78-75218
Printed in the United States of America.

1.9 8 7 6 5

Contents

CHAPTER 1

The year was 1975.
The place
was a little village
near the capital city
of South Vietnam.

Mai sat
in her house.
She looked
out the window.
She thought
about the war.
She looked
at her village
and felt sad.
How long
could it hold out?

Just then she saw
Set coming home.
Set was Mai's husband.

Mai asked him,
"What news
do you hear, Set?"

"No good news,"
said Set.

"Tell me
what you hear,"
said Mai.

"All right.
I'll tell you
before the children
come home from school.
Please sit down."

Mai sat down.
She was ready
for bad news.

"I hear
that the North Vietnamese
are getting close
to the capital city.
Soon the city will fall.

Then the war will be over.
We must
leave the country now.
People in the capital
are already leaving.
Some are going out
by boat.
I hear
that American planes
are coming in soon.
They will take us out."

   "I see,"
said Mai sadly.
"If the enemy
takes over,
there will be
no place for us.
Maybe they will kill us.
Yes, Set,
we must go.
If we stay,
we might be killed."

   Set was sure
that was true.

He had worked
with the Americans.
Because of that,
the enemy
would try to find him.
And now most of the Americans
were gone.
Set would have to leave too.
He had no job now.
But he had saved some money.
He knew he might need it
to get out of the country.
He had known
for some time
that they would probably
have to leave.

"Yes, Mai,"
he said.
"They might
want to kill us."

Mai asked,
"But where
will we go?
What will we do?"

Set said,
"We will find a way.
We will go
to the United States.
There we can start
a new life.
We will try to forget
about this war
and what it has done."

"But Set,"
Mai said.
"What about
the children?"

"They will go
with us,"
said Set.
"We will all
stay together."

Thinking It Over

1. What do you remember
    about the Vietnam war?

2. If you had to leave your home
    fast, what would you take
    with you?

3. It is said that
    home is where the heart is.
    What does this mean to you?

CHAPTER 2

Mai and Set
told the children
about leaving home.
The boys were named
Vinh and Bao.
The girl was Thi.

They packed
only what they could carry.
They paid $45
for a ride
on a truck.
The truck
took them
15 miles to the capital.
It was a lot of money.
But they had to get there.

And so
the five of them
left their village.

In the city
they would try to find
a way out.
They gave up their home
to find a free life.
They would leave Vietnam
forever.

Things were very busy
in the capital city.
Everyone ran around.
The people knew
that the enemy
would soon take over the city.
It was
only a matter of time.
Some people
wanted to stay.
Some people
wanted to leave.
Some people didn't know
what they wanted to do.

Because Set
had worked
for the Americans,

they would help him now
to get out of Vietnam.
His family
could fly out, too.
They all got
some special travel papers
from the Americans.

Set's family was taken
to Tan Son Nhut.
It was an air base
near the city.
Many, many people
were there.
They were all waiting
for planes.

Soon everyone heard
that a plane
was ready for boarding.
Mai held on
to Bao and Thi.
Set held on
to Vinh.
Many people ran
toward the plane.

Mai and the two children
got on board.

Just then
the door closed.
Mai looked up.
Where were Set and Vinh?

"Set!
Set, where are you?"
Mai kept calling.
She looked all around.
But there were
so many people
on the plane.
Then the plane took off.
She could not find
her husband and her son.

Thinking It Over

1. Have you or
    someone in your family
    moved away from your
    "roots" because of war?

2. Is it easier or harder
    to make decisions
    when you are in danger?
    Why?

3. Have you ever
    had to pay more
    for something
    because many people
    wanted it?

CHAPTER 3

Mai and Bao and Thi
sat on the plane.
Mai looked out a window.
She saw her country
below the plane,
moving far away.

"Good-bye, Vietnam,"
she said to herself.
She was very sad.
She had lost
her country.
Now she had lost
her husband and son too.
She wondered,
What will we do?

She thought about
how nice Vietnam had been
before the war.
Her children

had never known their country
that way.
She thought about
her mother and father.
They had been killed
in the war.
She thought about
her old school.
It was gone, too.
She thought about
her house.
She would never
see it again.

Little Thi
was crying.
"Don't cry, my baby,"
said Mai.
"It's all right.
It's all right.
Your mother is here
to keep you safe."

But Mai was afraid.
She had never been
on a plane before.

She didn't even know
where the plane
was going.
She was leaving her home.
And Set was not
with her.
But she had two children
to care for.
They could not know
how she felt.
They must not know
anything was wrong.

She thought about
Set and Vinh.
It would be
so much better
if they were here.
Where were they?

Thinking It Over

1. Do you think
   children should know
   about their parents'
   problems?
   Why or why not?

2. How would you feel
   if you were Mai?

3. Have you ever been
   on a plane?
   What was it like
   the first time?

CHAPTER 4

The plane went
to a place called Guam.
It was far out
in the Pacific Ocean.
The United States
had an Army base
on Guam.
People from Vietnam
were taken here.
From there
they would go
to different places
in the United States.

Mai and her children
stayed in Guam
for two weeks.
They stayed
in old Army buildings.
The buildings were called
"Tin City."

Tin City was very dirty
and crowded.

We will make
the best of it,
Mai thought.
She tried
to keep the children
happy and clean.
She found pretty flowers
to put
next to the children's beds.

Mai met a woman
who knew some English.
She told Mai
what was going on.
The woman's name
was Oanh.
Oanh was 42 years old.
Her family
was there too.
There were 17 people
in her family.
She had a husband,
six children,

her mother and father,
and a brother and his family.
Oanh was a big help
to Mai and the children.

"Some day you will find
your husband,"
said Oanh.
"Maybe he came here
on a plane after yours."

Oanh went with Mai
to find out
if Set and Vinh
were in Guam.
Every day they asked.
But they
did not find them.

One day
Oanh heard some news
in English.
She found out
that the capital had fallen
to the enemy.
She told Mai the news.

"We will be all right,"
said Oanh to Mai.
"I just know it.
We will get help
from the United States.
We are war refugees."

Mai looked at Oanh.
Then she asked,
"What is a refugee?"

"A refugee is someone
who must leave his country
to be safe,"
said Oanh.
"A refugee lives
in a new country.
But a refugee
has no country.
We are
from Vietnam.
And we will live
in the United States.
But we are not citizens
of Vietnam
or of the United States."

"I never thought
this could happen to me,"
said Mai.

"No," said Oanh.
"I never did either.
But this is the life
we have.
So we will make
the best of it.
We will go on living.
We are lucky
we got out in time.
We are lucky
to be alive!"

Thinking It Over

1. What would you do
    if you had to live
    in a place like Tin City?

2. Would you have as much
    hope as Oanh?
    Why or why not?

3. What does it mean to you
    to be a citizen?

4. What has happened
    in your life
    that you thought
    could never happen?

CHAPTER 5

Oanh and her family
left Tin City
and Guam
at the same time
as Mai and the children.

They all went
to California.
It was another
long trip by plane.
They waited in California
for someone to find
a home for them.
They stayed there
for two weeks.

Then they went
to Pennsylvania.
It is a state
in the East.
There they were taken

to a place
called Fort Indiantown Gap.
There were long houses
for them to stay in.
"The Gap"
was an old Army base.
It had been opened again
for the Vietnamese refugees.

Americans took care
of the Vietnamese
at the Gap.
They gave them food and clothes.

Mai picked out
some nice clothes
for Bao and Thi.

Still, Mai
could not find Set.
She and Oanh
asked about him
every day.
Oanh helped Mai
learn to say,
"Do you know

about my husband, Set?"
But the answer was always,
"No, we are sorry."

There were
many, many people
at the Gap.
Even if Set were there,
it would be hard
to find him.

One day
Mai asked Oanh,
"How long
will we be here?"

"We have to wait
until they find sponsors for us,"
said Oanh.

Mai asked,
"What is a sponsor?"

"A sponsor
is someone who helps.
A sponsor

will give us a home
in the United States.
A sponsor will help us live
until we have
some money."

Then Mai asked,
"Where are the sponsors?"

"All over this country,"
said Oanh.
"They may live
near the Gap.
Or they may live
far away.
A sponsor can be
one person
or a group.
Many times
a sponsor is a church."

"I see,"
said Mai.
"Will a sponsor
take care of
a whole family?"

"Oh, yes.
You will stay
with your children,"
said Oanh.

Mai took Oanh's hand.
She was happy.
This is
what she had wanted
to hear.

Thinking It Over

1. How far away from home
    have you been?
    Did you like being away?
    Why or why not?

2. How would you feel
    if you were a refugee?
    (Or, how did you feel
    when you were a refugee?)

CHAPTER 6

Mai and her children
were at the Gap
for three months.
Many things
went on there.
Some were good,
and some were bad.

Oanh's mother
got sick.
Soon she died.
All the people
at the Gap
had a funeral for her.

But there were teachers
for the people
at the Gap.
Bao and Thi
learned some English.
They played

with the other children
and learned
new games.
They ate a lot of good food.
They were happy.

New refugees
came in every day.
One man had brought
a TV set
all the way from Vietnam.
Many people
brought money.
But the money
was no good to them
in the United States.

And everyone brought
a different story
of how they had left Vietnam.
Mai made
many new friends
at the Gap.
They learned English together.
They sang songs
from home.

But still
there was no news
about Set.
The Americans
didn't know
where he was.
Mai thought
about him and Vinh
all the time.

At the end of August,
Mai got some news.

"We have found a sponsor
for you and your children,"
said the Americans.
"Your sponsor
lives near here
in a city
called Lancaster.
You will go there in one week."

Mai told the news
to Bao and Thi.
They were sad
to leave

their new friends
and move again.
Mai was sad
to leave Oanh.
But she was happy
to be starting a new life
in the United States.
She didn't know
what was in store.
But she was ready.

Thinking It Over

1. If you were far from home,
    what is one story
    you would tell about home?

2. Have you ever missed
    someone who was far away?
    What could you do about it?

CHAPTER 7

The sponsor's name
was Mr. Baker.
He came in his car
to pick up Mai
and her children.

"Hello, Mai,"
said Mr. Baker.
"I am so happy
to meet you.
Come with me
to my home."

Mai said good-bye
to Oanh.
"I will miss you,"
they said to each other.

"Maybe I will see you
again sometime,"
said Mai.

"I hope so,"
said Oanh.

Mai liked Mr. Baker
right away.
He had a kind face.
She could tell
he liked the children, too.

Mai and the children
got into Mr. Baker's car.
They drove
to Lancaster.
They did not say much
because Mai
did not know much English.
But Mr. Baker knew
how Mai felt.
He knew
she was sad
to leave Oanh.
He knew
about her husband, too.

"It will be very hard
to find a sponsor

for Oanh and her family,"
said Mr. Baker.
"Her family
is so big.
But I will try
to find one for her
who lives
near us."

"Thank you very much,
Mr. Baker,"
said Mai.
She had a smile
on her face.
Her life was hard,
but she always smiled.

Thinking It Over

1. How would you feel
    if your life
    were in
    another person's hands?

2. How would you get to know
    someone in the United States
    if you spoke no English?

3. What is nice about having
    a small family?
    What is nice about having
    a large family?

CHAPTER 8

Mai and her children
lived with the Bakers
for a while.
Mr. and Mrs. Baker
had four children.
Bao and Thi played
with them.

Mrs. Baker found out
about a school
where Mai
could learn
more English.
The children
started school too.
They went
at the same time as Mai.
They all learned
more English.
Soon they were able
to talk to the Bakers.

One day
Mr. Baker gave Mai
a letter.

Mai asked,
"This came for me?"
She was so happy
to get the letter.
It was from Oanh.

Mr. Baker
had found a church
to sponsor
Oanh's family.
Now Oanh was living
in Lancaster too.
Mai was very happy
to have her friend
in Lancaster.

Mr. Baker
had more good news.
"I have found
an apartment for you,"
he said.
"It is in the city.

It is small.
But it will be
your own place to live."

Three days later,
Mai and Bao and Thi
moved into the apartment.
Mr. and Mrs. Baker
gave them beds,
a table, chairs, lamps.
They also gave them
things for the kitchen.

"All this is yours, Mai,"
said Mr. Baker.
"I will pay the rent
until you can get a job."

Mai thought
this was all very nice.
But she didn't like
taking so much
from the Bakers.
She just smiled
at Mr. Baker.

Thinking It Over

1. If you were Mai,
    would you rather live
    with the Bakers
    or in your own apartment?
    Why?

2. Why do *you* think
    Mai was glad
    to have Oanh in Lancaster?

3. Do you think
    Mai should pay back Mr.
    Baker for his help?
    How could she do it?

CHAPTER 9

Life in Lancaster
was very different
for Mai.
She was poor.
She had no husband.
She had no job.
She was living
in an American city.
It was a long way
from her little village
in Vietnam.

Mr. and Mrs. Baker
were very good to Mai.
They helped her a lot.
Still, Mai wanted
to be able to do things
for herself.
She didn't think
she would ever
see Set again.

Mai was
a very smart woman.
She did many things
with her time.
She went to school.
She learned a lot.
She put ads in
Vietnamese newspapers
in the United States.
She hoped the ads
would help
find her husband.

Soon she started
to look for a job.
In school
she had learned
how to fill out
a job application.
She learned
how to use a bus.
And Mr. Baker
sometimes took her
in his car
to look for jobs.
But it was hard.

Back in Vietnam,
Mai had worked.
But without knowing
enough English,
it was very hard
to find a good job now.

"Mr. Baker,"
she said.
"I want to work.
You are very good to me,
but I should work.
I will take any job."

She found an ad
in the newspaper
for a job
at a chicken farm.
She wanted to work,
so Mr. Baker
took her there.

"This is not
very clean work,"
said the man
at the chicken farm.

"We kill chickens here.
Then we get them ready
to sell.
But if you want a job
helping us,
you can have it."

"I want the job,"
said Mai.

"OK, then it's yours,"
the man answered.

Mai started work
the next day.

Thinking It Over

1. Why did Mai take the job
   after the man said
   it wasn't nice work?
   Would you take it
   if you were Mai?

2. What can you do
   with your time
   if you have no job?

3. What life skills
   are important to know
   (besides filling out
   a job application
   or using the bus)?

CHAPTER 10

The man was right.
It wasn't very nice work.
But it wasn't too bad.
Mai was a good worker.
After a few days,
she didn't mind
working with the chickens.
She saw other workers
killing the chickens.
She was happy
she didn't have to do that.
Her job was
to clean out the chickens.

She was making
enough money
to live on.
This was what
she had wanted.
Yet something
was missing.

Every day
she thought of her home
in Vietnam.
She could never forget
how pretty
the village had been
before the war.
The war
had made the country
so ugly.
She missed home.
But she knew
she would probably be dead
if she had stayed there.

I wonder
if Set is still there,
she thought.
I wonder
if he is still alive.

One day
Mai got home
from work
late in the afternoon.
The children

were playing.
She was glad
they were doing so well.
They learned English
very fast.
They made friends
with American children.
She heard them
laughing outside.

She went to see
if she had any mail.
No letters.
Wait—
there was a letter
way in the back
of the box.
She pulled it out
and looked at it.
She knew the writing.
It was Set's writing!

"Bao! Thi!
Come here!
There's a letter
from your father!"

It had been a year
since Mai had seen
that writing.
She read the letter
out loud
to the children.

Thinking It Over

1. Why do children often do
    better than adults
    in a new place?

2. How do you feel
    when you hear from a friend
    after a long time?

CHAPTER 11

"Dear Mai,
dear Bao, dear Thi.
I am alive and well!
I read your ad
in a Vietnamese newspaper
here in California.
I was so surprised
to see it!

"My heart
was never so sad
as the day I saw
your plane fly away.
I never stop thinking
about you.

"You left
on the last plane
that day.
The next day
the Americans took Vinh and me

to an Army base
in the Philippines.
It was very hot,
and the base was crowded.
Both Vinh and I
got very sick.

"I got well again.
Little Vinh did not.
He died
in the Philippines.
It was the end
of the trip
for our dear son.

"Later I was sent
to an Army base
in California.
Now I am living
with an American family.

"We must
be together soon.
California is beautiful.
But you are
more beautiful.

I will come to you
as soon as I can.
We will be
together again.
We must be
together again soon!

　"There is no need
for you to write.
I will be with you
before a letter
can get here.
Wait for me.

　　"My love,
　　Set"

Thinking It Over

1. If you were Set,
   would you ask Mai
   to come to you
   or would you
   go to her?
   Why?

2. Set is all by himself.
   Mai is with two children.
   Which one has
   a better life?
   Why?

CHAPTER 12

Mai was so happy.
A year ago
her world had fallen apart.
Seeing Set again
would be a dream come true.
Mai went to work
every day that week.
But Set was
on her mind—
not chickens.

Eight days went by.
Still no Set.
I hope he is all right,
thought Mai.

It was Monday morning.
Mai got up
for work.
She looked
out the window.

The sun
was just coming up.
The street
was almost empty.

But way down the street,
a small man
was walking slowly.
Mai wondered
if it could be Set.

She got dressed
very quickly.
She combed
her long, dark hair.

Then the doorbell rang.
The man
walking down the street
had been Set!

Bao and Thi
got to the door first.
They were not sure
who the man was.
They were very small

and had not seen their father
for a year.
Set picked up
both of them.

"Daddy!"
It was the first time
little Thi
had ever said that word.

Set was so happy
he couldn't speak.
Then he saw Mai.

Mai stood
at the top
of the steps.
She watched the children and Set
together again.

Then she walked down,
one step at a time.
Set just stood there.
He smiled.
Then he let the children down
and ran to meet his wife.

They didn't say a word.
They held each other close.
They didn't want to let go
ever again.
They held each other
to make up
for every day
of the year gone by.

Then little Thi said,
"I'm hungry!"

The whole family
went into the apartment.
Mai called
the chicken farm.
She stayed home
from work
that day.
The family ate
a big breakfast together.
They had so much
to talk about.
Set wanted to know
everything that had happened
to Mai.

After she told him,
Mai asked Set,
"How did you get here?"

"I found rides
all the way
across the country,"
said Set.
"But that is all
in the past.
Today we begin
a new life together."

There was nothing but hope
in everyone's heart.

Thinking It Over

1. What do you do
   when you are waiting
   for something to happen?

2. What do you think about
   most: yesterday, today,
   or tomorrow?

3. Do you think
   things will work out well
   for this family?
   Why or why not?